Advice
for
Young
Writers

Also by Lewis Burke Frumkes

Favorite Words of Famous People

How to Raise Your IQ by Eating Gifted Children

Mensa Think Smart Book: Games & Puzzles to Develop a Sharper, Quicker Mind (co-author)

Name Crazy: What Your Name Really Means

Manhattan Cocktail

Metapunctuation

The Logophiles' Orgy

Advice for Young Writers

Marion Street Press

Portland, Oregon

Published by Marion Street Press
4207 SE Woodstock Blvd # 168
Portland, OR 97206-6267
USA
http://www.marionstreetpress.com/

Orders and review copies: (800) 888-4741

Printed in the United States of America
ISBN 978-1-936863-67-9

Library of Congress Cataloging-in-Publication Data pending

For Amelia Beatrice

ACKNOWLEDGMENTS

I'd like to thank all the contributors who generously shared their wisdom with me and Adel Manoukian who helped me immensely with the transcriptions.

CONTENTS

INTRODUCTION

When you want to do something really well, you go to those who do it well for advice, or so I believe. Want to play the harp well? Go to a great harpist for lessons. Paint well? Go to a great painter for instruction. Do mathematics or physics? Go to the great mathematicians or physicists for direction, or inspiration. It is not an accident that scientific wunderkinder gravitate to The Institute for Advanced Studies at Princeton, or The Courant Institute at N.Y.U, or to M.I.T. or Cal Tech to study with the masters. However this does not mean that a talented writer can imbue you with the very spark of talent that he possesses, though perhaps he may be able to show you ways in which you can nurture your own gift and bring it to flower. The great photographer Steichen first tried his hand at painting... saw that he fell short when compared to the painters he most admired so he turned to photography instead and became a giant.

Over the years I have been both a reader and a writer... and enjoyed both activities. Some years ago I started *The Lewis Burke Frumkes Show*, a radio show on which I would interview high-profile people in the arts and sciences, people whom I admired, or whose work I admired. Among them were geniuses, wits, artists, and poets at the highest levels... Nobel Laureates, Man Booker Prize-winners, Pulitzer Prize-winners, National Book Award-winners. Out of genuine curiosity I asked many of them what advice they would give to young writers starting out, and to a one they would share their thoughts with me. Among the authors who may be familiar to you, Sandra Brown, David Mitchell, and Tom Wolfe gave me advice. Walter Mosley gave me advice, Jonathan Safran Foer gave me advice; Ann Patchett and Ben Okri gave me advice, and Orhan Pamuk gave me advice. Arundhati Roy, and A.S. Byatt gave me advice and Jerzy

Kozinski in what was to be his last interview before he died gave me advice. New York Times columnist Russell Baker gave me advice and Erica Jong gave me advice. Yann Martel, Tobias Wolfe, and Daphne Merkin gave me advice as did the great Ray Bradbury, Colson Whitehead, Lee Child, and Nicholas Sparks. Linda Fairstein, Alan Dershowitz, Pete Hamill, Alan Furst, and A.M. Homes gave me advice. Even The Amazing Kreskin, Cynthia Ozick, Bruce Jay Friedman, Jimmy Breslin, Jules Feiffer, and Mary Higgins Clark gave me advice. Please include talented writers of today such as Yiyun Li, and Patricia Lockwood, along with Calvin Trillin and Chuck Palahnuik. I was delighted by these interesting re-sponses, and in turn I am happy to share their thoughts with you in the hopes that these seminal thinkers and authors may be able to help you, or at least encourage you to find your own talent and express it in writing. This then is the origin and *raison d'etre* for *Advice to Young Writers*. I hope you enjoy it and profit from it. And perhaps after you have read it you will pass it on to other young writers you may know... adding a little advice of your own.

—Lewis Burke Frumkes

January 5, 2015

New York City

Advice
for
Young
Writers

Diana Abu-Jabar

Novelist and winner of the American Book Award for Crescent

I think you have to find your process and honor it. For me, I read Stephen King's *On Writing* and he talked about being very disciplined and writing at the typewriter or computer every day for hours at a time. And for a long time I felt very bad about myself because I didn't do that. I am not someone who can sit down and just plug away for hours without stopping. I am very fragmented. I like to eat and socialize and go outside. And I still was writing and I was still producing, and I kept beating myself up because I wasn't doing it in this traditional way. And I would just tell people, find a way to make writing an important part of your life and however you do it, that's what's right for you.

Discipline, Process, Self-Determination

Warren Adler

Author of the novel War of the Roses *and short story collection* New York Echoes

But an avid reader does not a writer make. If I had the writer's bug, I didn't know it until I came face to face with my freshman English teacher at NYU, Dr. Don Wolfe. Yes, teachers do inspire. It is, indeed, a noble calling and a great teacher and mentor is a lifetime gift.

Education, Inspiration, Mentors

Diane Akerman

Poet, essayist, and naturalist and author of
One Hundred Names for Love

Follow your curiosity. It's no use going into bookstores and saying, "I'm just gonna focus on being as well known as..." That's very appealing. But if you follow your curiosity and what you're most passionate about, you will have an interesting life. And also you can't help but have that flow into what you're writing. So probably then you will be successful, but even if you're not, you will have a very intense and beautiful experience of life. So that's it—instead of focusing on the end product, focus on the process, and being as present as you possibly can.

Curiosity, Experience, Process

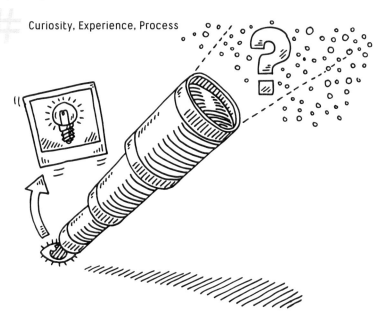

Martin Amis

English novelist and author of Money *and* London Fields

" I would tell them two things. These are the only useful pieces of advice I've come across. First, write about what you know. Don't write tremendously elaborate fantasy. Be specific, write about what you see, don't necessarily write about yourself, write it about the world as you know it. That is part one.

Part two: just keep writing, keep going, get drunk with power when you write. Dismiss anxiety. There are no rules involved.

Creativity, Freedom, Perspective

Russell Baker

Two-time Pulitzer Prize winner and author of Growing Up

You begin writing by finding someone you're terribly enthusiastic about and really like that person. After you have plagiarized five hundred good writers, a style of your own has emerged.

Imitation, Style

David Baldacci

Best-selling novelist of Absolute Power *and* The Finisher

Don't say, "I should take the next two years to sit down and write a novel." Take a few years and learn how to write well. Learn the craft. Don't finish anything. Read everything you can and practice. Try to build a character to the point at which you can see the person and how he moves and acts. Practice writing dialogue until a reader would say it sounds like two people talking.

Then, start with a short story, and after you've done that for a few years, try to construct a novel that is a major work. Look at it long term. You may have raw talent as a writer. There is a big difference between having raw talent and having the skill it takes to write a book. You have to have patience and perseverance. Don't try to do too much too soon.

Craft, Dialogue, Pacing, Patience, Talent

John Banville

Irish novelist and winner of the Man Booker Prize

Harry Pinter recently said in an interview, "When I first put on my play only six people came, three of them walked out and I was ignored by the other viewers. But I stuck to my guns and kept at it." And that's my advice. Keep at it. If you're not good enough, you'll quit.

Perseverance, Rejection

Dave Barry

Pulitzer Prize-winning columnist and
humorist and author of over 30 books

First of all it's hard because you almost have to have another job when you start. I mean, I was teaching writing courses and didn't even consider humor writing as a career until I was thirty-five and had a mortgage, a child, a dog... The thing is, no one in the writing side of it is looking to hire you as a humor writer, so you almost have to start as a freelance person somehow, even if that means you are working for a newspaper and on the side you are writing a column. But very rarely can you start out and suddenly become a salaried, full-time humor writer.

People want to see that you really are funny long-term and the only way to prove that to them is to write a lot of funny stuff before they've hired you. So if you're just starting out and you want to write humor pieces, the best thing to do (you know everyone hates to hear this but it's the way to do it) is to start writing stuff and sending it off, mostly to small publications that publish humor... Probably easiest is that *Writer's Market*. And then you will find that you get paid very little, very late, for a lot of work for a while; this is paying your dues, and everyone pretty much goes through that (well, I did). For the longest time I made twenty-two dollars a week writing humor. So it's very competitive, it's very tough to get started. It's not an easy way to make money, it's not an easy field to get into. I'm not saying people shouldn't try, they certainly should. But... they should not have illusions and they should certainly have a day job.

Writers are not editors and yet writers are always sending stuff to other writers, which is kind of silly because first of all, writers are usually terrible critics—they're sympathetic because they know how hard it is. And second of all, they don't buy anything. So you writers out there: don't send stuff to writers, even if you admire them, because it's really not going to help you. Send it to someone who's really going to be honest with you and tough on you, and above all who represents the true market.

You can't say, "I'm funny. I'm a humorist" if no one laughs at you.

 Day Job, Honest Criticism, Humor Writing, Paying Dues

Louis Begley

Acclaimed novelist and author of About Schmidt
and Killer Come Hither

The piece of advice I would give is don't. But if they want to persist, I think one has to remember that writing is done word by word and sentence by sentence. And what you put down on the page has to be well made. So one has to be always reading—reading and rereading what one has written down. And improving it. Correcting it until one is absolutely sure that when you shake it, it doesn't rattle. Too much self-criticism is probably a bad thing. But not enough is even worse. So I think that the writer has to accept the hard work that writing represents and the hard work that is required in order to produce something worth reading.

Hard Work, Revision, Self-Criticism

Melinda Blau

Journalist and author of the best-selling Baby Whisperer *series*

Practice, practice, practice... it's one of the few professions you get better at with age. And they can't faze you out; well, some of the magazine editors look like they're my grandchildren. It's really practice, but you cannot be a prima donna and think, "Oh, this is perfect." The art of writing is rewriting and that's another piece of advice.

Practice, Revision

Lawrence Block

Best-selling Edgar and Shamus-award winning
mystery author of over 100 novels

It's very hard to know because the business is changing so rapidly at an aston-ishing pace. As recently as two years ago I would have said, "Do not even think about self-publishing." Now I can't say that. Now that may be the best entry level method for a person. It's very hard to know and I got into the business so long ago, so there's a lot I don't know about what it's like now, but oh read a lot, think a lot, and the most important single thing I would say is: write to please yourself.

Reading, Self-Awareness, Self-Publishing

Stefan Merrill Block

American novelist and author of The Story of Forgetting
and The Storm at the Door

Go to law school. I really think only write if you absolutely feel you will be wasting your life if you are doing anything else. You should only write if it feels absolutely imperative, because it is so difficult and the career of a writer maybe from the outside resembles permanent retirement, but from the inside it feels like anything but. And the energy that books require is profound. There's no way you could be a writer without it coming out of a deep urgency to produce the things, but if you do feel that you have to do it, then just wholly commit yourself to it and just take a crappy job and lock the doors and do it.

...

The advice would be, to any writer, is that you should not worry about your career. You should worry about your craft and if you throw yourself wholly into your craft, have faith that a career will follow and actually in a lot of ways, the career is a distraction. There's a real freedom to the absolute poverty I was writing in and the sense that everything was just echoing into oblivion unless I did something with it. It freed me to really experiment, and so now I still feel free but I guess I feel a kind of pressure to produce another work.

Career, Energy, Faith, Persistence, Urgency

Ray Bradbury

Legendary best-selling author of Fahrenheit 451
and The Martian Chronicles

" I think Bill Maxwell, who was my father's editor and in many way my mentor, told me that everybody should write, that it's as natural as breathing. And I feel that way very strongly. I think that writing, and I don't mean necessarily successful writing, but sincere writing is like prayer, and I think when we write, we struggle with our understanding of the world... We're not improving the world whether we're published or not, so I think everyone should be encouraged to write. I do feel the heartbreak of those who have a lot of trouble getting published, but I think publication should be their secondary, not primary, calling.

\# Sincerity

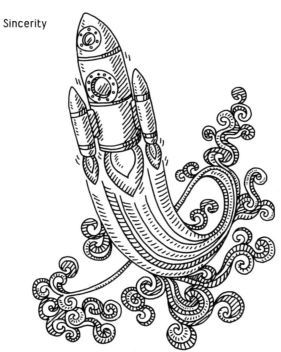

Arthur Bradford

O. Henry Award-winning American writer and
Emmy-nominated filmmaker

Get rid of your television set... I like television a lot, I enjoy watching it, but it's very hard to get work done. Anytime you could be watching TV is time you could be reading or writing, so I think that's a good step if you're serious about it.

Distraction, Focus

Barbara Taylor Bradford

Iconic international best-selling novelist and
author of A Woman of Substance

Not to give up, because I think it's so easy to become discouraged. Before I wrote *A Woman of Substance* I had always been a journalist and written nonfiction. I one day decided, "I want to write fiction, I always wanted to do it and I'm going to start trying my hand at it." I started but did not finish four novels; each one I kept but put aside. And imagine, I might have never attempted the fifth because I was discouraged, not because I'd been rejected but because I didn't like what I'd done and I thought I couldn't do it. And then one day I had that idea and I battled through and I wrote *A Woman of Substance*. And I think to believe in yourself. "This above all: to thine own self be true," said one of the world's greatest writers, Shakespeare. Keep doing it.

Perseverance

Jimmy Breslin

Pulitzer Prize-winning journalist and author of How the Good Guys
Finally Won *and* World without End, Amen

Just write!

Focus

Sandra Brown

Author of over sixty New York Times *bestsellers*

Well first of all, you have to read. Constantly, and continue to read, even if you're reading a book you're not particularly liking, you need to read it and try to analyze and determine why you're not liking it, what is it about it that you're not liking.

Secondly, you have to write. And you can join critique groups, you can go to seminars, you can do workshops, you can study and talk about it, rub elbows with people who do it, but there really is no shortcut I know to sitting alone all by yourself for hours, days, weeks, months at a time in front of a keyboard putting down words. And that's what it requires, and I love days like that, that's my favorite day, to sit in a room all by myself with my characters for uninterrupted periods of time and tell my story. And unless you're willing to do that, I would say get another profession because it requires that solitude and that compulsion to sit down and tell the story.

 Reading, Solitude, Storytelling

Edna Buchannan

American journalist and crime mystery novelist

"
You have to write, really be persistent, write all the time, never give up. Read when you're not writing because reading is so important... read, read, read; write, write, write and don't give up.

Persistence, Reading

A.S. Byatt

English novelist, poet, and Man Booker Prize winner

The first is to keep reading. Read everybody. I've met a lot of people in writing groups, and one of the things they tend to say is, "I don't read other writers in case it destroys my originality." You will not be original if you do not read other authors' writing. People who do not read other people's writing are all the same.

The second piece of advice is always to stop when you are in the middle of something that you know the next bit of and are excited by it. Then, you can take it up again the next morning. That keeps the continuity going, which is one of the real hassles. If you stop when you know what you are going to write next, then you do not have a blank page facing you.

The third is to carry a notebook everywhere. Write down things that you see. I never write things down about myself. Play with the language. I do not have any advice about professional forms and structures. Walter Moseley is about as far from me as you can get, but I have learned things about rhythm from him. People should read very widely, and then digest what they've read.

 Journaling, Originality, Pacing, Reading

Chelsea Cain
Best-selling thriller author

It is kind of twofold. One is to learn to write when you don't want to. And two
is to learn that writing takes a little bit of mad self-delusion. You have to
convince yourself that you can write a book. And that's crazy. And I, like always,
write a book a year. And I'm under contract, right? And half way through that
process I get to a point where I am like, "shit, they're gonna find me out," that
I'm this fraud, I can't write a book. But I have to just convince myself, "no, this
is perfectly normal, people write books all the time, there's bookstores full of
books, libraries full of books, and I will write a book, and I will write all these
pages, and it'll be this high and people will want to read it," and you know,
that's insane. But I think it's so easy to get paralyzed by self-doubt and by the
voices in your head and you just have to push them away and you just have
to convince yourself that you can do it, like, "I can write a book." I think what
really separates the people who are really able to do it from the people who
aren't is self-delusion. It is a beautiful mad skill.

Discipline, Self-Confidence, Self-Doubt

Susana Case

Poet and author of Salem in Séance

Do it, don't do it, do it, don't do it. Do it, don't do it. I mean you have to figure out what you want because you have to really love it, and you have to be willing to do a lot of work that you're never going to get paid for. Unless you're a comedy writer on TV. Then you get paid.

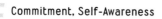 Commitment, Self-Awareness

Maud Casey

Calvino Prize-winning author of The Shape of Things to Come

I would say read voraciously. Because that's going to be your best teacher. And then I would also say, and this is something the writer William Gay once said in an interview and it always stuck with me, and that is "cultivate the ability to reside in bafflement." Which is to say get comfortable with being confused and with mystery. Because writing is not a straightforward enterprise, and so there has to be a little bit of patience with yourself and patience with the work.

Patience, Reading

Michael Chabon

Celebrated Jewish-American novelist and Pulitzer-prize winning author of The Amazing Adventures of Kavalier & Clay

"I would say that you must read constantly, and fairly indiscriminately within the limits of literary writing. I think you need to read all over the map. Male writers, female writers, from this country, from other countries. I think you should always be reading, especially when you are first starting out.

I think it is important to try and imitate writers whose work you admire. You can imitate them as slavishly as you'd like, and it will never come out being a perfect copy. And I think it's in the difference between your attempts to copy between your literary heroes and the actual writing of those heroes themselves; whatever that difference is, is sort of the kernel of what is going to make your writing eventually unique.

I would say that you have to give it up right away if you don't like being by yourself. Almost all of what it consists of is sitting in a room with the door shut all alone for hours. And if that sounds awful to you then forget about it. And then I would also say that you have to have a time every day, the same time every day that you do your writing. Even if it's only for an hour. You need to have a regular schedule and stick to it. And you never have to worry about being blocked. I've never experienced block.

 Imitation, Reading, Scheduling, Solitude, Uniqueness

Susan Cheever

Guggenheim Award-winning American author and memoirist and author of A Handsome Man

"Essentially the writer's life is to make up a fiction for yourself that makes it bearable. It's hard to know what it takes to write a book. Clearly it takes more than the ability to write.

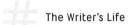 The Writer's Life

Lee Child

Best-selling author of the Jack Reacher *novels*

I would say, it is very simple my advice—it's three words: ignore my advice. Because like I said, the only thing that would make a book work is if you personally individually believe in it one hundred and ten percent. If you get into a situation where you're sitting at your desk and you say to yourself, "I really want to do this but I heard Lee Child say 'that's a bad thing to do' or Stephen King says 'do it later in the book' or this other guy says 'don't do it at all.'" If you get into that situation, you are lost because nothing happens by committee. If you want to do that thing, you do it. As long as you believe in it, then the book will have a beating heart and that's the only requirement for potential success. The book has got to be alive on arrival, not dead on arrival. If it's alive on arrival at the starting line then maybe you won't get anywhere. Maybe you will. You can't tell, but at least you'll have done your part.

 Focus, Persistence, Self-Determination, Success

Mary Higgins Clark

Legendary best-selling author of more than 24 suspense novels

I think the best advice is to write… The best thing to do is to practice it, and also to take writing courses. I think that's very important because then you get feedback, and you're in it with other people and if you have a good teacher who can guide you I think that's really important—to take writing classes and to do it!

Education, Practice

Jennet Conant

Best-selling author of Tuxedo Park *and* A Covert Affair

"The best stories are the ones that haven't been told before, and it's all yours to tell. So if you've got one, write it.

 Uniqueness

Jeffrey Deaver

Edgar and Nero Award-winning mystery/crime author of The Bone Collector

Well, a couple of things. One, I would say, find what genre or style of writing excites you, what gets your blood boiling, and stick to that. Never try to second guess the marker, for instance, and say, "Hmm, let me think, I've never read a book about a boy wizard, I don't like wizards, I don't like fantasy, but I'll bet I can make a million dollars writing, *Fred, the Boy Wizard From Brooklyn*." Don't do that.

I would say you should structure an entire book before you simply sit down and start writing, assuming you want to be a novelist. If you want to write a short story, structure the short story. But have an idea where you're going to go. A writer is a craftsperson in the same way that an engineer who builds airplanes is a craftsperson. We don't want to get in an airplane when the builder said to the raw materials manufacturer, "Give me some steel, give me some aluminum, give me some plastic, and give me some wires, and I'm just gonna see how it goes." No, you do the blueprint first. I do very extensive outlines, probably in excess, I probably don't need to outline as much as I do. But to an aspiring writer, come up with an idea and then before you write a single word of it, get yourself ten, fifteen, twenty pages of outlines so you know where the story is going to go and don't start before that.

And I guess the third thing I would say is just don't worry about rejection. You're going to be rejected. Writing is a very subjective thing, and the best book in the world is going to be rejected by some of the best editors in the world. Just consider rejection a speed bump; it's not a brick wall.

 Craft, Passion, Rejection, Structure

Nelson DeMille

American thriller novelist and author of The General's Daughter

It sounds like trite advice, but you know, a little less TV, a little less Internet. You gotta read. I mean, like our generation, who read for entertainment, not just pleasure. There was no entertainment around. If you're out there playing ball with the boys, when the day went night, you read. There was one TV in the house and your parents were watching their show and you didn't wanna sit there with your parents. I did a lot of reading and I think all my generation did a lot of reading. I say, read, read, read.

If you really wanna be a writer, write, write, write. It doesn't matter what you're writing, it's like exercise, there's no such thing as bad exercise. Yeah, you can do bad writing, and they say practice makes perfect. Well, perfect practice makes perfect, but you gotta read, you gotta write. People talk about it forever and they think in terms of movies and I think they think in terms of the result rather than the writing.

It's a very, very tough occupation, believe me, as you know. You sit there alone in a room as you tell yourself stories hours at a time, without human contact, and the real world starts to get more distant to you in some ways, so you gotta break out of that. The writers from the thirties who we know had more of a life than the armchair writers of today, I am thinking of the Hemingways and the Steinbecks—they had experiences: World War I, World War II, the Depression, the Roaring Twenties. Whatever it was, they lived history. A lot of us today, unfortunately, have never been outside our comfort zone.

I have, fortunately and unfortunately. I spent three years in the Army and one of those years at Vietnam. Vietnam in some ways liberated me. It made me kind of want to write the great American war novel. Why, I have no idea, but I never really did write it, but it kept me out of that kind of class. I was middle class like everyone else, suburban, nothing in my life I thought I should have

needed to write about. But if I started the Vietnam novel, then I started thinking of other things and the action adventure, the Walter Mitty stuff that we all
think we'd like to. ...You know, if you want to be a writer, you've got to have an
imagination. People talk about the writing process but obviously, it's so obvious
that you need an imagination. If you're a good storyteller, but you kind of got
yourself with those buddies at the bar, you sit down at the cocktail party and
tell a story and it makes sense and it's logical and your mind is quick. If you
can master the English language and how to write it, then you know you can be
a writer.

 Focus, Imagination, Reading

Alan Dershowitz

Legendary American legal titan and author

Write only what you know about. You must write things that you've experienced. I know, when I write, first of all, I separate out the art of thinking with the art of writing. I think it through first, then I write. I only write about things I feel completely comfortable with. Things I've experienced. Things I know more than my reader knows about. I don't try to say, "This is an interesting subject. I will do research on it now and then I will write a book about something I now know nothing about." You can't get comfortable with a subject just by doing the research.

Experience, Expertise, Research

Joël Dicker

Swiss novelist and author of
The Truth About the Harry Quebert Affair

It's a tough question but the one I could give from my very short and limited experience is just keep trying. Keep working harder. Keep rewriting, keep redoing the same and the same and the same until you're absolutely sure you're giving your best. Because I really think that writing a book is not about being better than another person but it's just like giving the best of what you can do at some point, at some moment, in a text. There are a lot of people who tell me, "I try but I don't know, I'm not sure." So keep working on it, keep trying. It is a very tough job. It is, and I think that people just need to give it more time.

 Patience, Persistence, Revision

Paul Dickson

Non-fiction author covering American English
language and popular culture

Get up in the morning, and you have two options: sit down at the machine and you either write "the" or "a" and you're good for the day.

 **Daily Practice**

Lou Di Palo

Author of Di Palo's Guide to the Essential Foods of Italy

I always say to people "follow your dream." Making a living, having all the pleasures of life—a fancy car, a big apartment, yes it is important but follow your dream and sometimes you'll reach a point in your life where you'll look back and you'll think, "Gee, I really had a satisfying moment" and at that point if you feel that you need to commit yourself to put that down on paper. Not so much for your self-satisfaction but to document for your future, for your future generation, and for people around you to have them say, "I feel good about how Lou Di Palo talks about his life through his work. I feel good about my life and the way I work and I want it documented as well." My advice is take the time, write it down. Today it's very easy to self-publish if you want to self-publish, or it doesn't even have to be published. Write it for yourself and have it for your future generations to read.

Self-Expression, Self-Publishing

James Ellroy

Noir international best-selling author of
L.A. Confidential *and* **The Black Dahlia**

Don't write what you know. Chances are you're gonna know life is not worthy of fiction. Explore your imagination, write the type of book that you love to read but you think no one else is writing.

 **Imagination**

Anne Enright

Man Booker Prize-winning Irish author of
The Gathering *and* **The Forgotten Waltz**

Look at the world. You don't have to write about the world, you don't have to write naturalism. It doesn't matter what; you can be writing genre fiction, you can be writing meta-fictive conceptual work. You can be writing extremely quotidian naturalistic work. None of these categories matter. What matters is the need you have to say this thing that cannot be said in any other way. I think some people, not students, but people I know who are writing books for the first time—they panic and turn around and say it's really hard. And I say, "oh really?" There's nothing I can do about that, it is hard. It's hard for every writer. It technically gets easier, but toward the end of a book, people get assailed by a feeling of the everythingness of it. That they're presenting everything they have, and they're not; they're presenting these pages, these sentences, which make a certain kind of sense. I would say to writers that it's largely a problem of mood management. Your mood is not the book. The book is on the page and you're outside of the page stomping around, having your mood.

 Mood Management, Observation

Linda Fairstein

Best-selling author of the Alex Cooper *crime novels*

The first piece of advice is read. Just read widely. Read things you're not used to reading to learn language and to learn how it's used and how good stories are told. And you know, try it. But write every day, write something every day, a couple of paragraphs, a journal. The procrastinators, the people who are able to convince me with their questions that they're never gonna write, are the people who never sit down with pen to paper or at the computer and just keep putting it off and putting it off and researching or "I have my homework to do." We all have second jobs. I mean, there aren't many of us with the luxury to sit down and write a novel. We all do other things and in my case, the work was in the new expression "twenty-four/seven." I mean those crimes came in day and night. You've got to find the time and write some words every day.

 Daily Practice, Language Skills, Reading

Jules Feiffer

Pulitzer-prize winning American syndicated cartoonist

 Don't let your judges define you.

Criticism

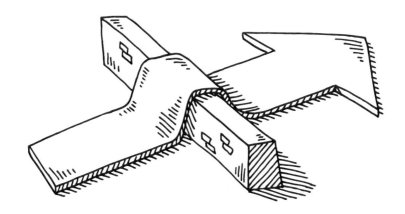

Amanda Filipacchi

Novelist and author of Nude Men, Vapor, *and* Love Creeps

Try to find a way of writing that you find fun. This is very challenging (I'm not sure I've found such a way yet). The more fun you find writing, the less strong your willpower needs to be to get yourself to do it.

In addition to the obvious—which is reading fiction—immerse yourself in everything having to do with trying to become a writer. Read writing magazines such as *The Writer*, *Writer's Digest*, and *Poets & Writers*. Read books on the craft of novel writing. Read interviews of writers (*Paris Review* interviews are great) and author biographies. Take creative writing classes every chance you get. Though it's far from essential, get an MFA in fiction writing if you can. It's inspiring and energizing to be surrounded by people who all have the same passion and are striving for the same goal. And the deadlines can be helpful.

Read John Steinbeck's *Working Days: The Journals of The Grapes of Wrath*. It's his diary entries at the end of each day, describing how hard that day's writing had been. It's a comforting companion to your daily writing routine. I've given a copy to all my writer friends.

Writing a first novel is daunting (all those pages!). So force yourself to write a novel in a month (ten pages a day). Even though that novel will probably be very, very bad, and your mother might say something like "I wouldn't show this to anyone, if I were you," it will give you confidence.

Then, write a novel in two months (five pages a day). It will probably still be very bad and this will depress you greatly, but you'll have gotten the message: stop writing a certain number of pages a day and start writing a certain number of hours a day. Focus on quality. Filling "all those pages" is the least of your problems.

Take all this with a grain of salt. It's what I did, but in my twenty-five year career as a published novelist, I've only written four novels.

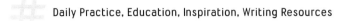

Daily Practice, Education, Inspiration, Writing Resources

Joseph Finder
Best-selling American thriller author of
High Crimes, The Zero Hour, *and* The Fixer

"I do talk to a lot of writers because I do sort of feel that it's one of the responsibilities of an established writer to help the younger ones, because there's no network for that. It's not like when you're in a corporation, when you have mentors who tell you what to do. There are no laws. There are no rules, no one tells you.

Well, a couple of things I tell writers is that they have to be stubborn and yet listen to people, take other people's advice that you respect, that make sense to you. I think that the most successful writers are not necessarily the best writers but are the ones who are the most persistent, that are actually stuck in there because it is so easy to be discouraged. There are so many ways to not get published. And it can be hard, but you've got to basically stick with it.

 Perseverance, Persistence

Boris Fishman

Award-winning journalist and author of A Replacement Life

Stay in the game. Half the trick is not dropping out. Find ways to stay in the game.

 Perseverance

Jonathan Safran Foer

Award-winning author of best sellers Everything Is Illuminated
and Extremely Loud and Incredibly Close

First of all, I would say, don't try to become another Jonathan Foer. There's enough already. I think the best piece of advice I ever received was from Joyce Carol Oates. She was my mentor, I guess. She was a teacher of mine in college, and was the first person to ever give me any reason to think I was a writer and has always encouraged me most often, just with truth rather than support. You know she will tell me when things are bad, really bad. She tells me things are bad more often than good, which is exactly what people need.

She once said to me the most important quality that a writer can have is energy. It requires an infinite amount of energy to keep going and energy against criticism. Energy against self-doubt, and also just on the page level. You want every page to be full of energy, for life to be coming through on every page. There's no reason to write unless you are absolutely working at the top of your game, trying to express every last thing about yourself and about life. And I know when I finished this book I thought, I don't know if I can do it again, if I'd have energy. And now I'm doing it again, and I'm sure I will feel out of energy soon.

 Criticism, Energy, Mentorship, Self-Doubt, Truth

Richard Frances

*Science writer and Clinical Professor of Psychiatry,
New York University Medical School*

Use your full brain power when you write. Include your dreams, expand your awareness, listen to your soul, and through your writing heal your own and the world's sorrows. But do it sober. Don't cheat or harm yourself with booze, LSD, hallucinogens, or cocaine. While too many writers have shortened brilliant careers with self-destructive addictions, this is a path to be avoided rather than emulated or romanticized. If you succumb to the above, seek help quickly and avoid damage to your gifts. You will be a better writer for it. Mental illness is not necessarily an impediment to great writing, nor is it a necessity to have suffered, and its treatment usually improves productivity. Through it all you need to love and take good care of yourself.

If you choose to write about science, be informed and know that dissemination of new science is crucial to translating the benefits of discovery to the bedside in health care and to a public awareness of the importance of research in all the sciences. Be a critical thinker and reader and make sure the evidence for what you say is carefully weighed. The best science writers can make the most complicated discoveries and concepts understandable to a lay public.

If you can't grasp facts, write fiction or poetry. Trust your imagination, feelings, and intuition. Seek new directions and get out front ahead of worthy causes. The world is a writer's oyster and the possibilities for writers limitless. For too many writers suffering from "writers block" the "excellent has been the enemy of the good" and self-doubt and perfectionism can slow productivity. Without the freedom to fail, no writer will take the risks needed to be great.

Don't be afraid, develop a work ethic, be eloquent and clear, and enjoy rather than be tortured by the process. Hang out with great artists and scientists and listen and talk to people high and low. Don't be surprised if it takes awhile for your full talents to come to fruition or to be recognized and don't be deterred by failures. We all have them. Beware vanity, ego, excessive self-absorption and whenever possible avoid becoming boring. If power, fame, and wealth come your way, use them with compassion and wisdom.

Finally as Nike says, "Just do it!"

Addiction, Ego, Science Writing, Self-Doubt

Dick Francis

International best-selling British crime writer

To know your subject. You've got to know your subject. Most of my books are set on the racing scene, or the equestrian scene; I know that scene pretty well. But the other things I incorporate—photography and computers and merchant banking and semi-precious stones, painting. You've got to research those subjects and know them well. It's no good writing about things if you don't know them.

Informed Perspective, Research

Bruce Jay Friedman
American novelist and screenwriter of Splash

 I can't improve on what Grace Paley said, which is "keep the overhead low" for one. I teach a course. I put a great emphasis on focus and a chilling piece of advice that one writer gave, I don't know who he was, that every word you write should be put on trial as if for its life. Now that's a tough thing to say to writing students, but I believe it has to be said and you can go through the works of the writers we all would admire and every word will stand that test, I believe.

Diction, Editing, Focus

Lewis Frumkes

Author of Metapunctuation *and* Favorite Words of Famous People

Write an opening line that is so commanding no one can put it down. Then follow it with a thousand others just as exciting. If you wish to be read, your writing must be lively. If you wish to get published, you need three things:

1. A modicum of talent. . . which I assume you have or you wouldn't be reading this.

2. Marketing skills. . . whatever the market you wish to reach—be it print, digital, audio, or something else, you must study the market and send targeted proposals or manuscripts.

3. Perseverance. This is most important. You cannot fold at the first sign of rejection. Legion are the people who give up at the first rejection of a story, essay, or poem sent to *The New Yorker*, *Harpers*, or *The Atlantic*. These people are failed without having given themselves a fair chance. They invariably have a trunk full of manuscripts in their attic. The successful ones persevere, believe in themselves, and submit until they are accepted. After twelve years of receiving rejections saying that your work is the worst crap the editors have ever received, I might rethink my mission. Architecture is a good field.

Marketing, Perseverance, Rejection, Self-Confidence, Talent

Roy Frumkes
Screenwriter and documentary filmmaker

This falls in the screenwriting area, but I assume most forms of creative writing could share each other's goodly advice.

Friend Ernest Tidyman, who wrote the screenplays for *The French Connection* and *High Plains Drifter*, as well as the *Shaft* novels, told me that each night he would decide what scene he was going to tackle the following day. He would then sleep on it, his subconscious would do the work, and in the morning, the scene would flow from brain to paper as if written while he slept and all he needed to do was transcribe.

I'm with Ernest in believing that creative writing comes from the subconscious more than from conscious effort. Unlike Ernest, I haven't had much problem with just sitting down each day and writing. True, I don't know where most of it comes from—It just comes. But when I do have difficulty it is with making sure my subconscious behaves.

Being an entity that organizes narrative more like the way we dream, the subconscious (Sub) will take any opportunity to thwart you from harnessing its powers. For instance, who hasn't been halfway through a script and suddenly thought of a far better idea for one? That's just mischievous Sub, trying to lure you away from the one you're working on. Laboring for that long in a linear fashion grows tiresome for Sub. But don't fall for it. Rather you should put this new idea down in a paragraph and file it away for future development. Then get back to the story at hand.

Likewise, if you're somewhere that you can be reached, then Sub will definitely resist you. Is there a telephone nearby? Are there roommates stirring in the other room? A radio or CD or an iTunes melody? No good. Find a place, for the time you have allotted to write, where you cannot be disturbed or found.

Which means leaving the cellphone at home. Some of you could more easily part with a limb. But it's got to be done.

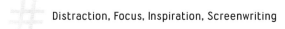 Distraction, Focus, Inspiration, Screenwriting

Keith Gessen

Novelist and journalist and co-editor of n+1

My advice—I think you meet a lot of people who think that you need to have connections, that you need to meet people. If you continue writing, you will meet all the people that you need to meet practically without leaving your house. And you will be given an opportunity to publish your work and the question is whether you'll be prepared, whether you will have read enough and thought enough and prepared yourself morally and spiritually for that. Those years in your twenties, you don't get them back, I feel, so if you waste that time trying to meet people, that will be the end of you. And I feel like I managed to use some of that time wisely, not as wisely as I could have.

Networking, Publishing

Shirley Gessner
Author of Charlaine

I think you can teach writing. I think writing is an instinct and an inherited talent. And I think if you don't have it you'll never be a good writer. You can write, but I think for any other artistic endeavor it has to be in you somewhere and has to come out. And if it has to come out, then you can become a writer. But if you don't have the talent for it, I don't think you can wake up one morning and say, "Okay, I have nothing else to do, I'm going to write."

Instinct, Talent

Emily Giffin

Best-selling author of Something Borrowed *and* Where We Belong

The advice to writers I would give is don't be intimidated by a finished book. I think there's something, like this mystique—that the book that you see in a library or bookstore and it's really just four hundred or so pages on your computer. There's a very thin line between the four hundred pages on your computer and what goes in that book. I think that's one thing. I guess along with that is don't be intimidated. Just get started. Don't feel like your first page that you write has to be the first page of the novel that's published. Just start writing.

Write what you love. Don't worry about what's commercial, what'll sell. Don't try to find someone out there who you think you're exactly like and pitch yourself that way. I think that can help in a query letter to agents. You know, "This is a combination of 'so and so' and 'so and so' and I like to think of myself as a modern-day 'so and so.'" But don't be afraid to be utterly original and follow your own voice and not worry about what's going to sell. Obviously I think all writers would say, "Write a lot and read a lot." I think that's probably universal writerly advice, right?

Confidence, Originality, Reading, Voice

Carol Gilligan
American feminist writer and ethicist and author of In a Different Voice

If you love it, if this is what you really, really love, if this is what you feel compelled to do, do it, try it. I mean, I think I'd say what I've said to myself which is, it really is like walking off a cliff. You can't know unless you start, and yet it's the most deeply, deeply satisfying thing I've ever done.

Know what you know; really, deeply know what you know. In a sense, looking for the voice under the voice including your own. That's hard; they sound very simple.

Faith, Satisfaction, Self-Awareness, Voice

Gail Godwin

Guggenheim fellow, novelist, and author of The Perfectionists

Read, read, read. And second of all, write about what really, really attracts you, what interests you even if it's something you dread. And then, after you've written it, look it over and be your own worst critic before you show it around too much. Unless you're so lucky to have friends and you can meet with them and you all do a mutual lemon squeeze.

 Passion, Self-Criticism

Myla Goldberg

American writer and novelist and author of Bee Season

Be persistent. Work hard. You have to give yourself structure. The thing about being a writer is no one is going to make you clock in and do the time, and no one is going to wait for you to finish that thing. So you have to structure your own life. You have to be disciplined.

Going to school won't give you that discipline. I know people who go to MFA programs and they leave without that discipline. And they say, "Well, I'm thinking about going for a PhD in creative writing" and like, no. Go write. Go get a life somewhere and write. So discipline, persistence. Read constantly because your best teachers are going to be the books that you read. And be prepared for a lot of rejection but don't let it squash you. As long as you want to do it, keep doing it. And do it for the love of actually doing it, not for what you think is going to happen, what you think you're going to get, because probably you're not going to get much.

Discipline, Love, Persistence, Reading, Rejection, Structure

Arthur Golden

Best-selling author of Memoirs of a Geisha

 For me as a teacher, the thing I've always tried to do is pass along what I can about fictional technique. And I think there is a body that can be learned of information, not outside information, but there is such a thing as fictional technique that every writer has to master as best he can.

Education, Technique

Barbara Goldsmith

New York "Living Landmark" and author of Obsessive Genius

Norman Mailer once said that when he got to be about forty he got tired of punching people who say, "I have a great story;" that a writer is not a conduit for a story, that writing is a craft. And it's at least as difficult as learning how to play the piano. And that if you want to be a writer just write. And I tell this to my kids when they were very young, and they are all pretty good writers: start anywhere! You don't know where to start? Start in the middle!

 Craft, Initiation

Francine Du Plessix Gray

Renowned author of Them: A Memoir of Parents *and literary critic*

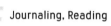 Keep a journal. Keep a journal and also read, read, read."

Journaling, Reading

Dan Greenburg

Humorist and author of the Max Segal *thriller series and the best-selling children's series,* The Zach Files

If you're going to get a career in writing, it's important to note that you may have some success, but then there's a lot of other stuff that you have to plow through before you can be successful again. So, for you "fledgling writers" out there, stay with it.

\# Perseverance, Success

Lev Grossman

Best-selling author of Codex *and the* Magicians *books*

I tell them to read everything. Nothing irks me more than an under-read writer. Just read everything you can get your hands on. I tell them never to give up. Generally speaking when writers can give up they should give up because they haven't got that engine inside them which just forces them to keep going. So I tell people never to give up. It took me fourteen, fifteen years to really feel like I found my voice and see some success. So you can't expect to hit it right off.

 Reading, Perseverance, Success, Voice

Pete Hamill

New York journalist and thriller author

Become yourself, and the way you learn how to do that is work. Write every day, write when you don't feel like writing, write when you're tired, write when you think you have nothing to say, write very day. Keep a journal if you're not writing for a newspaper, go out of town and get a job at some small newspaper just to be able to pick up that fearlessness I think you need.

And be humble. Humble yourself before great writers, but never stop reading. You gotta read until they cart you off to the cemetery. And the reason for that is that you are constantly as a writer, particularly if you are a productive writer, pulling water out of the well. You must continue to replenish the well, and the way a writer replenishes a well is through reading to begin with. And experience the other arts, of music and painting and sculpture; knowing that all of those things feed the apparatus.

 Authenticity, Daily Practice, Humbleness, Reading

Deborah Harkness

Historian and author of the All Souls *trilogy*

I think there's a lot of trying to figure out what they should be doing in terms of the market and what editors are buying and what's selling and what's not working. Look, when I sold *A Discovery of Witches*, it turns out there were actually whole pages of agents that would say, "No vampire books." If I had been paying any attention and listened to that, I wouldn't have written this book. So I think that what you have to do as a writer is you absolutely have to tell the story you need to tell. And people may say that the world doesn't need that story, they may say that the world doesn't want that story, they may say that there's no market for that story. Maybe some of those things are true, but the bottom line is, if it's the story you have to tell, you have to tell it before you can move on to something else. Even if it's in your desk drawer. And writing really is a daily practice. It is not a thunderbolt of inspiration from on high. Two pages a day for a year, is a seven hundred-page book. Sit down and think, can I write two pages today? That's my job as a writer.

 Daily Practice, Self-Expression

Colin Harrison

*Senior editor at Scribner and celebrated New York author
of* The Finder, Risk, *and* Afterburn

My advice would be a couple of things, and I have given this advice before in workshops over the years. My advice would be to read an enormous amount, write an enormous amount, don't kid yourself, get serious about it, dig in, dig in in those years between twenty and thirty because that's when you really must develop very quickly. If you say you don't have time to write, but you want to write, you're telling yourself a fib. Ask yourself, "Am I watching too much TV? Am I on the Internet too much? How am I wasting the time that I should be using writing and developing?" If you're honest with yourself, you'll see that there really is time to get the work done. I know, because I've worked full time forever and I get it done.

One more thing: you must really learn the craft. You must learn what a scene is. You must learn the mechanics. I get submitted novels almost every day and nothing turns me off faster as an editor when it's clear that the writer doesn't really know what a semicolon is, doesn't understand an em-dash, doesn't understand what the reader wants as opposed to what the writer wants to say, and it's a process. I think it takes almost ten years to bake as a novelist and you might as well get started, and you might as well go at it as hard as you can.

\# Commitment, Devotion, Process

Josephine Hart

Irish writer and author of Damage

I would say that it has to feel to you that this is irresistible. Otherwise, don't start. It's rather like acting. If you do not feel that this is an utterly irresistible, important, and good thing (you may be dealing with evil subjects but good thing to do), then you will approach it with humility. I mean, Martin Amis used to say to me that the god of art is a god, you come and you lay your offerings before him or her and humility is all, so that is the way to approach it—with enormous humility and believing that this is my offering and that it is important and to the god of art and it's not to do with your ego. It's not to do with anything else other than an offering to the gods of art who have really made life possible for most of us.

 Ego, Humility, Passion

A.M. Holmes

Winner of the Women's Prize for Fiction and
author of The Safety of Objects

My advice would be, is to in fact, write and not to wait until you're ready to write, not to wait until you're in the mood to write, not to wait until you have an idea of what you're going to write because that is a very fleeting thing and you need to make the habit of writing and the practice of writing and you need to show up every day to that half empty page or that blank page.

Daily Practice, Mood Management, Persistence

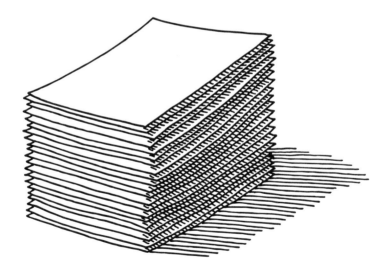

Katherine Howe

Best-selling author of The House of Velvet and Glass
and Conversion

I think the most important thing is to be selfish of your time. I think it can be tricky when you want to write to insist on the time necessary to do that writing because there is always something else that has to be done. Whether it is an errand that needs running or, you know, even a fun activity that your friends want you to do. It is important to insist on the time necessary to write every day and it is important also to surround yourself with people who understand that that is important because being as selfish as one needs to be with writing time can be tricky. And not everybody understands it as a worthy use of time so I think that's the most important thing.

 Devotion, Discipline

Evan Hunter (AKA Ed McBain)

Prolific crime fiction author including Blackboard Jungle, The 87th Precinct *series, and screenwriter for* The Birds

I was going to say, go rob a bank instead, but to be serious make sure you really love it. Make sure it's what you really want to do more than anything else because you're gonna be all alone with the computer or the typewriter or the lying pad or the lipstick, all alone. And it's just going to be you and whatever you have to say. And make sure you really want to do it because it's not easy.

 True Calling, Solitude

Rowena Husbands

Celebrity photographer and author

Follow your dream. Do not let anyone tell you that you cannot do something. If you're passionate about something, do it. Step out on faith. I would say learn your craft. And if it's a natural thing, just hone in on it. Do what you do and love what you do.

Faith, Passion, Perseverance

Siri Hustvedt

American novelist and essayist and author of The Blazing World

 My advice is this: there are no rules in art. There are no rules in writing and you find your own way. That is my best advice.

Freedom, Self-Expression

P.D. James

The doyen of English mystery novelists and
author of The Children of Men

I would say develop your use of language by reading good writers, not so that you can copy their style, because writers need to develop their own style. But when you meet an unusual word, get used to it, write it down, find what it means. Try to increase your vocabulary, because a good writer needs a good vocabulary. You need to read, you need to practice writing, and you need to go through the world with all your senses alert to what is around you: the natural world, the world of men and women, the world of work, and for a writer, nothing that happens is ever wasted. It's developing that sensitivity to life, and at the same time trying to hone the craft, thinking of it as a craft.

Craft, Reading, Sensitivity, Style, Vocabulary

Tama Janowitz

Award-winning novelist and author of
Slaves of New York *and Andy Warhol protégé*

There's not really any reward in it. Even the writing itself isn't that fun ninety percent of the time. So unless it's your vocation and you're driven to do it... it's the ones that keep at it and keep at it that end up being dead writers who wrote twenty books that no one read.

Drive, Pointlessness, Vocation

Ha Jin

*National Book Award-winning Chinese-American poet
and novelist and author of* Waiting

I think patience is essential for a writer... you need to be patient and you need to be stubborn... stick with it!

Patience, Stubbornness

Celia Blue Johnson
Author of Dancing with Mrs. Dalloway

I would say based on my research of all these great writers, that they had so many failed ideas. Just keep trying and keep looking for the right idea. Keep writing because even the great writers stumbled and what set them apart from everyone else is that they picked themselves up and marched on. There's a great anecdote about William Faulkner who sent a manuscript called *Flags of Dust* to a publisher and the publisher wrote back to him and basically said, "I think that a writer needs to have a story, and they have to be able to tell their story, and the problem is you don't have a story." And William Faulkner sat down and said, "Okay, you know what, I'm not gonna write for the publishers. I'm gonna write for myself." And he wrote *The Sound and the Fury*. So never give up.

Criticism, Inspiration, Perseverance

Richard Johnson

Legendary Page Six columnist for the New York Post

The best stories are the easiest to tell. When you are really having trouble writing, it might be because you don't have a good story. If it's too complicated to pitch to an editor in two sentences or less, it's probably too complicated for your readers.

My other bit of advice is to get the words out. The words can be changed later, but you can't rewrite unless you write first. You need something to work with—even if it's crap. Keep those fingers moving.

 Storytelling, Persistence

Erica Jong

Award-winning novelist, essayist, and poet and author of Fear of Flying

I believe that if you're a writer, you produce a shelf of books, and that when you're eighty you have a book for every several years of your life. And some of them may be great hits and some of them may be misses, and some of them may be experiments that didn't quite pan out, but that you go on producing one book after another, and that each one is an experiment of a different sort and they are a chronicle of your life. And that you take risks. And that you don't crap out at some point and find a formula, and opt-out of the struggle to produce original works of art.

Chronicle of Life, Experimentation, Perseverance

Nancy Davidoff Kelton
Author of Writing from Personal Experience

Years ago, I started to write a mystery. I outlined it in a notebook and described my characters on cards, having everything I needed. Except excitement. And joy. And a compulsion to tell the tale. My body showed up at my desk each day, but my soul was in Lost-and-Found. I continued writing, anyway, until I faced a problem too big to ignore.

I couldn't figure out who did it. In my book.

That was a clear enough signal to resume writing what I loved and still love: the personal essay. That is what engages me. It is also what—at several colleges and with different course names, including *Writing from Personal Experience*, the title of my book—I teach.

To make a personal essay come alive, it should have the following two components:

1. Emotional involvement: Woody Allen says eighty percent of life is showing up. When it comes to writing—creating anything, really—I think it's more like one hundred and ten percent. You've got to show up fully, care what you are writing about, and put your heart into what you say. Something from within should be impelling you forward. If you are not excited or eager to tell the story, imagine how your readers will feel. They'll be bored or napping or elsewhere.

2. The arrival at some basic truth: As a result of the experience, something should become clear to you. You should reach a new level of understanding, come to an "aha". This should not sound like an Aesop fable or a greeting card, but good writing has revelations. Universal truths. In an artful way, deliver the truths your readers subliminally know so they can say, "Yes, that's how it is. I've been there, too."

The difference between self-revelation and self-absorption is the difference between "aha" and oy vey! When you reveal yourself honestly on the page, you not only can craft a good personal essay, you get to hang out with your best self.

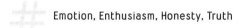 **Emotion, Enthusiasm, Honesty, Truth**

Susan Konig
Parenting humorist and author of
Why Animals Sleep So Close to the Road

"Get it down on paper. Yes. Old school. On paper.

Writing longhand is a physical act. You will remember what you wrote—because there is more muscle memory in actually taking pen to paper. When you write longhand, you tend to put more thought into what you are doing, as opposed to pecking away on a keyboard (or, God forbid, texting your next novel with your thumbs) which can become a mindless exercise. So writing longhand helps trigger other brilliant thoughts that you didn't even know you had and you won't need the seat with the charging station at Starbucks. When you write longhand, you can't delete the entire work with one click. And when the grid goes down—and it will because the zombie apocalypse is coming!—you'll have an advantage over all the other writers. All the other writers dependent on electricity whose brains are now being eaten by zombies.

I've written on receipts, envelopes, napkins, unpaid bills, more unpaid bill and, ultimately, on the back of collection agency notices. Hey, it's sustainable. When I forgot a pen, I wrote in eyeliner. I've written in the middle of the night, on the subway, standing in line at the DMV, and in the dentist chair between rinsing and spitting. Don't wait for your special "writer's time" in your special ergonomic "writer's chair" to type it into your special "writer's document" on your special "writer's Macbook/tablet/iPad"—get those brilliant thoughts down as they come in!

And don't edit your writing before you actually write it. Don't self-censor! Write it down no matter what your inner critic tells you. You can't edit nothing.

My stories about family reflect the familiar—no vampires, no boy wizards. With me it's all harrowing tales of backed-up plumbing, cranky teenagers, and man-eating raccoons roaming freely in the wilds of suburbia (well, they knock over your garbage cans...). I write about everyday annoyances. If they are so common, then why did I bother to write them down? The point is that I did write them down in a voice that is unique to me. That's what your readers connect with—your unique voice, captured on paper in the words you wrote down. So write it down on paper, before the zombies get here.

 Daily Practice, Journaling, Longhand Writing, Voice

Jerzy Kosinski

Polish-American award-winning author of Being There

I think I would imagine that anyone creative should be as creative as she or he can. Try to do it without advice of the others. Believe in yourself, in other words, a creative work is derived from the innermost conviction. If you submit it to the judgment of others, you are actually abandoning that very egocentric and idiosyncratic quest. This would be my lesson derived from thirty years of being myself. That if you want to be really faithful and truthful to everyone else, you have to be truthful and faithful with yourself. Then, you cannot fail, but no filters and no intermediaries. Hence, write the whole book rather than one chapter. Don't run around asking, "Is it good or bad" because you should be asking only yourself and no one else. That's what I think makes a creative personality. The dependence on oneself. For good or bad.

Independence, Inner Conviction, Judgment

Elizabeth Kostova

Best-selling author of The Historian *and* The Swan Thieves

To read, to read voraciously, to read things many people have thought for one reason or another are great, to read inquisitively so that you're always turning the chair over and seeing how all the joints are put together.

And the other is to persevere. I think it's very difficult to keep writing. It's not so hard to start writing, it's not hard to write very well, but it's really hard to keep writing. I didn't publish a book for about twenty years, and I think a lot of young writers have very understandable illusions about that and how quickly they're going to reach a certain level of prose and/or can get published. And I think it's very important to set up one's life so this is a dedication.

Critical Reading, Dedication, Perseverance

Kreskin

Famous mentalist, television personality, and author of 19 books

It seems like a challenging time, because the publishing industry is in great trouble today. A lot of them have lost touch with communications, as far as PR is concerned. I know them well because of some of the major ones, and some of the books are now being printed, self-printed. And I want to tell you something: before, when you write your book, before you jump away and say self-printing is just too risky and so forth, a couple of extraordinary best sellers were done by people who self-printed their books.

My advice to you is this: some of the greatest writers of all time, including Mark Twain and so forth, did not make their living as a writer. They made it as a lecturer speaking about their books. You write something, if you believe in it for long enough, see if you can get someone to support you, get it printed. If you don't get it printed, you can still get it printed so long as you put it on paper. You will have something to look back upon because the one thing you need to learn today, which has never been the case in the history of mankind—even if you hid something, there are no secrets left on the face of the earth. Every youngster should be told this. Nothing left—it is a world that has never existed before. You send a memo to someone on the Internet and it may come back to haunt you sixty years from now, so if you write a book, put it in print because if it doesn't work now, it may work later on.

Public Speaking, Self-Publishing

Camilla Läckberg

Best-selling Swiss crime writer and author of The Ice Princess

 It's a lot about killing your darlings when you write. You have to distance yourself when you finish the manuscript and be able to let go of some of the stories you wanted to tell which is not quite necessary maybe to telling the main story, and you have to be able to kill your darlings.

Critical Editing

Dylan Landis

Journalist, novelist, and author of Rainey Royal

Don't stop. Hard work is more important than talent and it wins out. And you must read. And you must analyze what you read.

Analysis, Hard Work, Perseverance, Reading

Nam Le

Dylan Thomas Prize-winning author of **The Boat**

I always feel a bit uncomfortable answering these advice questions. I think if you appreciate the value of the time and space that you need for writing, and one of the best ways of coming to that appreciation is to work in a white-collar corporate office. I think it really does something.

Deprivation

Christopher Lehmann–Haupt

Former senior daily book reviewer for the New York Times and author of Me and DiMaggio *and* A Crooked Man

The only way to learn is to do it and to do it and to do it. It's a marvelous exercise, marvelous thing to do because there's no limit to how much you can grow, how much you can learn. After doing it for thirty years, I'm still learning new things about the language and about technique and about everything.

Skills, Technique, Writing Exercises

Elmore Leonard

One of America's greatest crime novelists
and author of 3:10 to Yuma

Read. You read and study what the writer is doing. Find a writer you feel you have a rapport with, and study the paragraphing, study the punctuation, study everything. I think the paragraphing is extremely important. Learn how to paragraph to keep the story flowing. Find out by experimenting how you write most naturally. You may be a traditional prose writer, an omniscient author whose words and descriptions are the most important elements. Or, like me, you hide behind characters and let them do all the work

Characterization, Paragraphing, Reading

Richard Lederer

Celebrated American linguist and author of
Anguished English *and* **Amazing Words**

My first piece of advice would be blow up the distance between who you are and what you do. Which I have done in my life, and that is why at my trombone birthday, seventy-six trombones led the big parade as you can see, and you know I have as much energy and maybe more than I had ten, twenty years ago. When you blow up that distance, you just have infinite energy, you never work a day in your life.

As with my kids, I was teaching at a church boarding school and they come tell me, "Dad, we want to play poker," and in Howard's case, Howard the Professor Lederer who got a start here in New York City, "I don't want to go to college, Dad," and in Annie's case, "Well, I'm about to get my PhD in psycholinguistics, but I'd rather play poker." You can imagine my response. Oh frabulous day, callooh, callay, I chortled in my joy, how much do you need, because you have seen your daddy do it and you're going to do it.

Second, find out what kind of a writer you are. I have always loved writin. I was the editor of my junior high school literary mag in inner city Philadelphia, and my high school newspaper. And I loved to write, but I noticed that I kind of sucked at narrative, dialogue, setting, all of those things that make fiction. And I could only do it well in service of nonfiction. I have always been an explainer. People ask, "Richie, when are you going to write the great American novel?" and the answer is never, it would be one of the worst. But for me the ideas are the heroes and I am addicted to learning that stuff. So that would be another piece of advice—what kind of a writer are you?

Another is, write every day that you can, just as your parents or your brother, sister, whoever, don't say, "Well gee, today I don't feel like going to the law office or working in the grocery store, the doctor's office," or whatever they're doing. As a writer it is a job, and as many days as possible, you want to contribute the bulk.

And another piece of advice is you're not going to write beautiful prose right off. James Michener, you know, said "I am an average writer but I am one hell of a rewriter." And he did pretty well.

 # Agelessness, Career, Practice, Self-Awareness

Yiyun Lee

*MacArthur Foundation fellow and
award-winning author of* The Vagrants

"My advice, I give this advice to my students all the time, it's not to pay too much attention to the fluffiness of the business or publishing, or don't read the hot young authors. I always ask my students to read the Russian masters. I tell them... I can take extra time talking with them if they could finish *War and Peace or Anna Karenina.*

 # Fads, Masters, Reading

Mark Leyner

Author of satirical fiction including Et Tu, Babe *and*
The Sugar Frosted Nutsack

Be as porous as a sponge as possible for what's happening out there.

Porousness

Sam Lipsyte

Guggenheim Fellow, novelist, and author of The Ask

Write constantly... I consider the first draft a sketch.

Daily Practice, Revision

Elizabeth Little

Critically acclaimed author of Biting the Wax Tadpole
and Dear Daughter

Unfortunately, I really do think the best advice is just to work your ass off. It's to put in the time. I look at things that I wrote when I was in my early twenties, and even though at the time I was like, "this is awesome," it is just a matter of learning and figuring it out; it's a skill. You know, I think there's this sense that it is something innate, an artistic talent with a lot of people that you can't teach or have or don't. But for me, it was, still up to this point, my first work of fiction (*Dear Daughter*), ever.

\# Hard Work, Talent

Patricia Lockwood

Critically acclaimed American poet and author of
Motherland Fatherland Homelandsexuals

I would look at whether you were really inclined to be pedantic or want to throw out rules entirely. And once you figure out where you're situated, then try and throw in something of the other, because I started, surprisingly, as a sort of pedantic grammarian-type person who is very high bound and very much believing that there are rules, and very much believing that the cops were going to come if I did not adhere to those rules. And what I needed to do was, you know, throw a little anarchy into the mix.

Now if you're an anarchist, then you need to fucking sit down and write sonnets for a little while. You just need to mix the two things together, but I think you have people who are inclined to become writers who are young, and there are of those two particular types and the pedants want to enforce the laws of the English language of good writing as they see them, and the other guys want to throw it all out. And so it is good to figure out which one you are, what your instincts are, and generally become better by inclining just a tiny bit in the other direction once you figure that out.

Grammar, Instincts, Style

Alison Lurie

Pulitzer Prize-winning author of Foreign Affairs

It depends so much where you're starting out from. I mean, nowadays, there are, I think, over a thousand graduate programs. When I was growing up, there was only one in Iowa. It's still there and there are still people going to it. But I think that just judging from the years that I taught in the graduate writing program at Cornell, it's much better not to go straight from college into a writing program. And we developed a policy that we wouldn't take anyone right out of college.

We wanted the best, we really wanted people between the ages of let's say 26, 27 on up to 40. People who had some life experience, who had something to write about, who had seen something of the world. And even if they were as good as John Updike, putting the sense of together, if they have no subject, what they'll come up with, they'll exhaust it quite soon. So we look for people who have life experience and have been places and have done things and could then use the kind of help that we could give them and that their fellow students could give them.

Education, Life Experience

James MacManus

Managing editor of the Times Literary Supplement
and author of Sleep in Peace Tonight

Don't give up; it is the obvious advice. Trust yourself, your talents, and never be afraid to tear up the first two or three drafts of anything you write because it always gets better.

 **Perseverance, Revision**

Yann Martel

Best-selling Man Booker Prize-winning author of
Life of Pi *and* **Beatrice and Virgil**

"Read. You cannot write without reading. Read widely beyond your particular interest. Play with language, try different kinds of things. Do write to be a writer. You have to write, let go of your expectations. It's extremely hard to succeed commercially in writing. There is a glut of fiction writing out there. It's not a reason not to do it, the world will tell you it doesn't need another writer; it does.

So keep at it. Do listen to your mother's advice: you should probably get a day job. If you're really serious about your writing, try to get one that doesn't expend your mental energies. I was a dish washer, I was a tree planter, I was a security guard.

 Day Job, Expectations, Reading

Patty Marx

Humor writer for Saturday Night Live *and* The New Yorker
and author of Starting from Happy

I would say it's always hard to think how to break into Hollywood, but how do you write? You just keep writing, you just keep writing and writing and writing and I think you'll reach your potential. I can't promise you that your potential would be high, but that's what I would do.

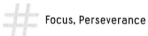 **Focus, Perseverance**

Trish Marx

Award-winning children's writer and author of
Touching the Sky *and* **Everglades Forever**

Find the emotion in your piece. An editor once told me she would accept a story about a clothespin if it had emotion in it, advice I used years later when writing about a one thousand year old mummy from Peru. I looked at the mummy, trying to find a connection. The archeologist unwrapped yet another layer of wool to reveal a basket filled with balls of yarn, under the mummy's arm. I flew back one thousand years, back to my grandmother's house and her basket filled with balls of yarn: red, green, brown, yellow. All there in this mummy's basket. Red, green, brown, yellowish. She was a weaver, a knitter albeit with thorn needles, she was a caregiver, a grandmother perhaps, I could tell her story with emotion.

Choose a story you can stick with when the waters turn murky, when you are done with it, revise again, take off your writer's hat and be brave enough to shout your story to the sky. There is an editor for every writer, every story, every interest, and if it has already been done, find a new and better way to execute it. Olivia lived before as Pippi. And there will be another spunky girl we will all love down the line. Believe she can be yours. Believe your story into life. Revise your story as you revise yourself daily by you brushing your teeth, changing your socks, and combing your hair. Write it to yourself in bed at night, carry it to the grocery store, the drugstore, wake up and write down passages that come to you in a dream, find the connection and reel it in. Now go write.

 Emotion, Revision

Peter Mayle

British Book Award-winning author of the best-seller
A Year in Provence *and* A Good Year

" Write. Well, you know it seems stupid and obvious but there's no tiptoeing around it. If you want to be a writer, write every day.

Daily Practice

Alexander McCall Smith

Legendary mystery author of the best-selling
The No. 1 Ladies' Detective Agency *series*

I'd say several things, one of which is to actually live and get experience. I think that really is terribly important. I think the biggest problem for authors setting out at a young age is the fact that really, he or she might not have actually seen much of the world. They may not have lived very much, and I'm not suggesting one has to go off to sea or climb Everest or whatever. What I'm saying is that they must actually just get experience of human life. Now there are some writers who manage to write extremely mature and insightful books in their early twenties without ever having done anything much, and they are much to be envied. But I think for most of us, we actually have to get experience under our belt. I think Hemingway made a point of that nature, and of course Hemingway was always rushing off to deep sea fishing and bull fighting and traveling and fighting in small wars.

Experience

Alice McDermott

American Book Award-winning author of Charming Billy,
At Weddings and Wakes, *and* A Bigamist's Daughter

Well, I guess the pat answer is read everything, especially when you're young.
Form your tastes, find out what's good because then you'll be able to know
when you're doing it... what you like, what means something to you. And the
other maybe not-so-pat part is, if you can do anything else and wake up in the
morning happy and go to bed at night contented, then do it. The only reason
in the world to be a fiction writer or a writer of literary fiction if I can call it
that is because you can and don't want to and mustn't do anything else. And
that will get you through this career.

 Drive, Reading, Self-Awareness

Ved Mehta

MacArthur fellow, essayist, and author of **All for Love**

 First of all, people often seek advice but nobody every follows advice. I think if a young writer came to me and said, "Tell me what I should do," I would simply say, be true to your talent, try to write, be respectful of fashions, currents of the day. That's all I'll tell.

Talent, Trends, True Calling

Daphne Merkin

American literary critic, novelist, essayist, and author of
Enchantment *and* **The Fame Lunches**

Read. First, read. In the courses I've taught, I'm always amazed when people write, want to write, and don't read because I don't know anyone who does who writes well. One way you learn to write well is reading a lot. And we write. I think because of the Internet and blogging and schmogging and emails, people don't revise, edit. In the end, my real advice is seduce. Writing is an act of seduction and if you don't seduce the reader...

 Editing, Reading, Seduction

Sue Miller

Best-selling author of The Good Mother,
While I Was Gone, *and* The Arsonist

"Everyone says it, read! But it seems to me if you've read a novel you take in by a sort of processes of literary osmosis—the way a book works, the way fiction works, the need for forward momentum and an arc. To me it seems as though a lot of young writers who I encounter... the notion of (writing) being a discipline is foreign to them. And I think if you read enough, you begin to see that others have disciplined themselves before you. With the marketplace as it is now, better to wait to be presenting something you're fully in control of, that you know how to do again. But I think reading primarily.

Discipline, Inspiration, Reading, Repeating Success

Grace Mirabella

Legendary Vogue *and* Mirabella *magazine editor-in-chief and author of* In and Out of Vogue

66 To try, in your own self to know, what it is you really want to do and not get taken by the frivolity of it.

\#\# Self-Determination

David Mitchell

Critically hailed best-selling English author of
The Bone Clocks *and* **Cloud Atlas**

Everything you need to learn about writing fiction you will learn and you will only learn by reading fiction. I think it's that simple. Learn from the masters. Work out why it is they can do what they do to you. Think about that but most of all—I didn't go through the creative writing course myself and I'm not knocking it, but I don't know much about it—but what I do feel is that the truest creative writing course are your first three god-awful, pretentious, self-regarding, really pretty useless and unpublishable manuscripts. Don't be discouraged by the fact that it's not an immaculate conception. I mean, it's like how could it be; it's like picking up a violin for the first time in your life and expecting to be able to zip off Helga's violin concerto. It won't happen, and it's an odd, pernicious myth to think just because you're literate, you can therefore spring fully formed from the brow of Zeus as J.D. Salinger. First off, you have to learn it, learn it, learn it. Pay your dues and be encouraged when you look back at what you wrote six months ago and you realize it's awful. That means you're making progress.

 Honesty, Masters, Perspective, Self-Evaluation, Setbacks

Walter Mosley

O. Henry Award-winning American crime writer and author of the Easy Rawlins *novels including* Devil in a Blue Dress

" If you love writing then write and write every day and continue to write and continue to write and try to find other people who love writing... And talk to them about writing and it'll take you somewhere, someplace great.

\# Daily Practice, Community, Persistence

JoJo Moyes

British journalist and best-selling romance novelist and author of Foreign Fruit *and* The One Plus One

Several things—one would be show up every day. Because if I had a dollar for everybody who told me they had a book in them but no time to write it I would be J.K Rowling, basically. You have to come do it, every single day. And be ruthless with yourself. Don't go for the easy stereotypical thing, just keep going.

 Daily Practice, Persistence

Annie Nova

New young writer and poet selected for this book

"Writing is hell. Being young is hell. Why would you ever combine the two? Because you'll need it.

Writing is our windbreaker as we meander with a fraying sliver of self-identity through a downpour

of uncertainty and angst. And you need to write to get through a storm as much as you need a

storm to write. Smooth sailing doesn't breed good writing, disillusionment and disaster do. We're

shaken by life and we write about it to shake our readers. So next time you're agonizing at the idea

of writing, remember, you're off to a great start! Lug all of that agony with you to the screen.

You're going to need every drop of it to write meaningfully. If you allow those flashes of gold

between your ears to die out, you won't be helping yourself or anyone, and then one day you'll

read them by someone else.

\# Agony, Inspiration

Audrey Niffenegger
Internationally best-selling author of
The Time Traveler's Wife *and* Her Fearful Symmetry

I think the best advice is simply to read, and read everything. And not be snotty about it, but to read anything they can get their hands on and to form their own opinions, and not necessarily just listen to us professors. And to keep going, because so much of what you do when you're young is practice, and some people get discouraged because their practice effort is not very good. But the people who get to do it their whole lives are the ones who persevere.

Critical Reading, Perseverance, Practice

Elizabeth Nunez

Trinidadian-American novelist, co-founder of the National Black Writers Conference, and author of Boundaries

 If you're passionate about it, you're going to continue doing it. So if writing is your passion, no matter what people say around you, you'll continue to do it and just continue to go forward. Smart people just want to write for themselves, and that's fine. But if you want to be published, you'll buy *Writer's Market* and go from A-Z and Z to A and back and forth until someone reads a letter and believes in you as much as you believe in yourself.

Determination, Passion, Persistence

Mike Offit

Author of the literary financial thriller **Nothing Personal**

There's this great phrase they always use, "follow your passion in life." I remember listening to your show years ago and you had the writer Linda Fairstein on, and she said the same thing I said, that her father had told her "please don't be a writer, do something else." And I think that if you feel the passion to write, you should do it. You should pursue it as a career, but I do think that life gives you experience and things to write about. Keeping that muscle and tone is an important thing but to really devote your life to writing creative fiction, you need some experience. Get out there and really experience life and write about it. And if you do do something else, like even on Wall Street I constantly wrote marketing pieces, I wrote long exercises on different topics so keeping that muscle in shape is an important thing, and to read. The best thing a writer can do is read.

Life Experience, Passion, Reading, Skills

Sidney Offit

American novelist, editor, and author of Memoir of a Bookie's Son

Five rules that will avoid insult, injury, and writers block:

1. Never ask a writer, "What you are working on now?"

2. Never ask a writer, "How's your book going?"

3. Resist saying, "You should write a book about that."

4. Never, never suggest, "You should sell that book to the movies!"

5. Never say, "That review was absolutely unfair to you!"

Determination, Focus

Ben Okri

*Man Booker Prize-winning Nigerian poet and novelist
and author of* The Famished Road

I suppose slowly as you get older and you learn to write, you find these people who, at first, make writing easy for you. They are those who don't terrify you by your achievement, at least they don't seem to; people like Tolstoy, seem so simple. Of course when you get older you realize that simplicity is damn near impossible.

I always say to people who ask me about writing, that short stories are the most difficult prose form and the most important; it's the secret of fiction. The novel is a great dream that comes out of that, but you need to have strength and structures in you and strength and mythic undertow and to have developed a very easy relationship with words, so that they don't sort of jump and shout at you but just swim and float quietly.

Don't be too enthusiastic about wanting to write, don't deify writing. It is not a god and it won't save your life. Love life. I think life is the greatest teacher. Books are just guides that come afterwards. Live intensely in books and forget them. You don't have to write every single day of your life. I think the most important thing you have to say, the thing that is the most obvious, is that your good ideas are really not so good. Be humble. Never stop learning. Never believe that you are good at what you do. Keep taking it apart. Listen to those who are much older than you. It is not necessary to always slay your fathers and mothers. I think you can sit at their feet, too, and shut up. And write slowly and live slowly. And don't think writing will bring you glory. It's not supposed to do that. The glory is being able to write something that someone else is moved by. And I suppose you should just live for beauty and live, live.

Humbleness, Intensity, Simplicity, Short Stories

Joseph O'Neil

Irish novelist and author of the critically acclaimed Netherland

First of all, I'm disinclined to give advice. I also feel that my basic duty is to discourage writers. I remember when I was a barista for ten years, and that's a very hard profession to get into—there's a massive attrition rate. For every ten people who qualify as baristas, only one gets to practice as a barista. And of those people, only a minority will in turn flourish, so it's a very tough profession. I remember going to these job fairs as a student and I'd meet these baristas and you'd say to them, "What do you have to say about the bar?" And they'd all say, "Don't do it, just don't do it." And I remember thinking, well, why come all this way to the university to tell people not to do it? And what they're doing effectively is deterring you, and if you're capable of being deterred by that kind of advice then you shouldn't be doing it.

So my feeling is, I would say to a young writer, don't do it. Why would you do it, nobody wants to hear from you, you're going to spend years, unless you are extremely fortunate, plowing a furrow in the wilderness, and it's going to get harder and harder and harder because guess what? You know if you have any artistic ambition, you know that you try to ratchet up every time, and it's really, really tough.

 Determination, Discouragement

Cynthia Ozick

O. Henry, PEN/Nabokov, and PEN/Malamud award-winning author of The Puttermesser Papers

Young writers should take advantage of all the plethora of periodicals there are now, which are enormously open to the young; and young writers should go and do reviews and journalism and publish early! Early publication gets confidence, late publication, such as I had, leaves you a butter knife the rest of your life.

Confidence, Publishing, Resources

Chuck Palahniuk

Award-winning best-selling author of Fight Club,
Survivor, Invisible Monsters, *and* Choke

Do not ever use thought words. Never write *think, believe, realize, agree...* if you use those at an extreme minimum, your writing will automatically become more effective, more dynamic.

Diction

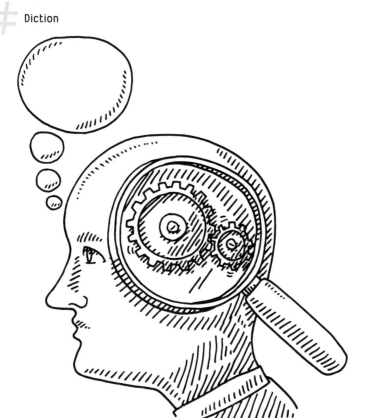

Orhan Pamuk

Nobel Prize-winning Turkish novelist and author of My Name is Red

Don't take any advice from old writers... You'll find your way.

Self-Reliance

Robert Parker

Dean of American crime fiction and author of the Spenser *novels,
the* Sunny Randall *series, and the* Jesse Stone *series*

It's the second most (used) advice in the world and they don't want to hear it. Write the thing and send it to someone who can publish it and they'll tell you whether they will or not.

Process

Ann Patchett

Best-selling Orange Prize and PEN/Faulkner Award-winning author of Bel Canto *and* State of Wonder

Don't fall in love with your own work, write a lot of it, and keep moving on!

Persistence, Perspective

Justin Peacock

Edgar Award-winning author of A Cure for Night
and Blind Man's Alley

"Read as much as you possibly can, and as broadly as you possibly can. To realize that a writing career really is a marathon and not a sprint—and I'm somebody who definitely put in my thousands of unpublished pages before I wrote a publishable novel. It took a long time to get it there.

You have to have faith and patience to respect the process of learning how to do it. Very few people can just sit down and write publishable fiction when they set out to, so you need to put in the hours.

\# Commitment, Endurance, Reading

Mona Pearl

Author of It's Not Over Yet

 Write What You Know??

What do we know about life when we are young? At 81 years of age

I am still learning, and I realize much of what I thought I knew was

only my perception. But perceptions are not always the truth. At any

age, write what you dream, what you feel, from your heart and your

soul, but write, write, write. This is your gift to the world.

Perception, Persistence

Marisha Pessl

Best-selling author of Special Topics in
Calamity Physics *and* Night Film

Approach it like plumbing—do it every day. Approach as if writing is your nine-to-five job, or if you don't even have that amount of time, it's something you have to complete every day. Take it out of the clouds, don't wait for inspiration or the muses to descend; simply know that plan to do it every day, even if it's for ten minutes.

\# Daily Practice

Christopher Reich

Thriller novelist and best-selling author of The Runner,
The Patriots' Club, *and* Rules of Deception

I have a few pieces of advice. One, read prolifically. Two, travel. Wherever you are, don't stay there. Go see the world and get some experience because I don't think you can write from a strictly American perspective, or let's say ethnocentric perspective. Just go out and have some fun and see the world and if you're like a novelist, if that's what you're aspiring, don't even start trying to write until you're thirty because I think you need that kind of perspective and experience and maturity that then lends novels the insight which makes them worth paying twenty-five bucks for. You know, people have to pay their dues and see things. So that's my advice—read, travel, and then of course, write. Don't wait for the muse to come, it never comes. Like Mark Twain said, the first rule of writing: apply back of pants to seat of chair.

Life Experience, Maturity, Reading, Traveling

Richard Reeves

Award-winning columnist and author of
Daring Young Men *and* **Infamy**

I would start a blog. You can be published. I sat in a little attic office I had for myself in New Jersey when I was a reporter for the *New York News*. I was desperate to write for a New York magazine or anybody on the other side of the Hudson River and I sent in idea after idea. The one I tried to sell the most never sold. I was a canoeist and I was to do a trip from the great swamp at Mars County to New York Bay thirty-five miles where you go from a total primeval world. The great swamp was primeval and at that time, it's gotten better, but at that time the deadliest water in the world. What happened in that thirty-five miles to destroy the essence of life.

I sent that to every magazine, magazines that no longer exist, what not. When I was lucky I got polite answers. Today if I were a kid I would write that and I'd get it on the Internet. There are enough sites. I know because I teach what the jobs are on the Internet, and I don't consider them very good. I mean, let's say the Huffington Post, which is an impressive operation, they're sitting there clicking other blogs and other websites, that's what they're doing to try and get out there three seconds earlier or something like that. Well, any kid walking by on the street there can get on to the *Huffington Post* or onto the *Drudge Report* or onto these other things so that I'd do the exact same thing I did, but it would be easier because you take out the middle man. I mean, the reason no one ever did my Passaic River story was that it would cost money to do it, but if I did it myself, it wouldn't cost a penny.

 Blogging, Self-Publishing

Graham Robb

Celebrated British historian and biographer and
author of The Ancient Paths

" Get a very large wastepaper basket and don't expect the first thing you write to be good… You have to rewrite it. Write and rewrite.

 Revision

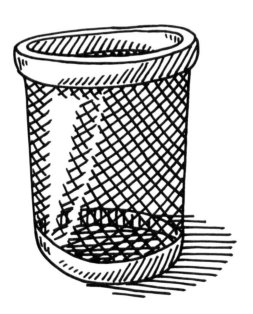

Arundhati Roy

Man Booker Prize-winning Indian author of The God of Small Things

I'm very suspicious of free advice. By free advice, I mean people who just advise people unnecessarily. Each person has to do it in his way. The way I worked was not to open my work up to opinions until it was finished. I worked for four and a half years without discussing it or showing it to anyone. Sometimes when you start soliciting opinions, your work just gets up and walks away. You have to be focused enough to know that you have to do it regardless of whether it's published or not, or whether it's successful or not.

 Focus, Perseverance, Privacy

Helen Schulman

Acclaimed American novelist and author of This Beautiful Life

You have to read and you have to learn how to read, and that doesn't mean reading for story. You have to read for strategy and tactic, and look at how words fit together in a line and what they do sitting next to each other, and how the lines fit together and how that forms a paragraph, and why it solicits the feelings that it does. And once you begin to understand that, you are working with a medium that can be manipulated and constructed and turned on its head. Then you can really begin to write, and I think that's like an awakening. It's like learning how to read all over again.

We have courses on "reading as writers" as do most programs now and it's really fun to teach because it's like the light bulb goes over someone's head, and suddenly they understand why they feel what they feel and how the writer set about manipulating them in a way to solicit that response. So I would say read and read carefully.

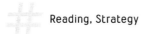 Reading, Strategy

Iris Smyles

American author of the semi-autobiographical
novel Iris Has Free Time

I'm reluctant to give any advice because I think part of me says like stop immediately. No, I mean, be brave, or I guess more realistically, you have to write, not just think about it. Many young writers want to be writers but they don't actually want to write, certainly for a while there was some confusion in my own case, it turned out writing is a lot more exciting but it's also a lot more difficult. So I would say be honest with yourself and figure out what you want and whether you're willing to do the work.

Bravery, Honesty

Lisa See

Author of the international best-seller
Snow Flower and the Secret Fan

The main advice I would give is that you should write something you're completely passionate about. That whatever it is, it's something you'll be living with for several years, let's say two years to write it, then it comes out in hardcover, then it comes out in paperback. And *On Gold Mountain*, for example, that came out in 1995. I'm still asked to go out and speak only on that book. You have to be really, really passionate about it, because, just like a marriage, there are certain days when you wake up and you think, "Ugh, yuck. I really wish I didn't have to see that person again." But you can feel that way about a story and so just like a marriage, there has to be this deeper, deeper love for the story, for the characters that will transcend those down moments. It's like the "in sickness and in health." Even when you're writing, there are some days you're in sickness.

Commitment, Love, Passion

Nicholas Sparks

Best-selling author of The Notebook *and* Message in a Bottle

Read a lot, read a lot, read with an eye toward what works, and what doesn't work, that's number one. Now if you're gonna be a writer, write. Once you pick a genre, learn the genre. Learn your genre, and then take the knowledge that you've learned and write it out.

\# Genre, Reading, Skills

Miguel Syjuco

Man Asian Literary Prize-winning novelist and author of Ilustrado

Revision is where writing is and don't give up... I didn't give up and it worked for me.

 Revision, Perseverance

Adam Thirlwell

Acclaimed British author of Lurid & Cute, Politics, *and* Escape

" Finish it.

Completion

Calvin Trillin

Legendary American columnist, humorist, and poet

I suppose there are cases of a piece being written too many times, too many drafts. Occasionally you see something that looks kind of precious and over-written. I would say that's so rare compared to the pieces you see that could've used four more drafts or something. That's not something to worry about. I think that generally the more you write the better the piece is. The hardest thing for me and probably for most writers is the structure of the piece.

How to get from A to B to C, and when I by chance know what the end of a piece is going to be, whether it's one of these columns or a reporting piece, it always buoys me because I know that I'm there when I'm there. But usually there are two different problems in a reporting piece. Even in a reporting piece like "The Clam Bake" I have a certain amount of information that I'm going to get in. Information is less important in "The Clam Bake" piece, than say, in a murder piece, but still a lot of it is organizing the information.

For a column, I start out with nothing and I don't know where I'm going to go. I'll start out with just an example, not realizing it's going to figure in the column very much. Turns out to be what the column is about, kind of by ac-cident, but in both cases I would say it's hard for me to count drafts because I do it in an odd way. A piece, they used to say, didn't write itself, wouldn't write as if it had some life of its own, but that's true in some ways. Occasionally you sit down and you just write a column and you've got to clean it up here and there but it comes out. That's not the way it usually happens, and also that's not necessarily the way it happens for the ones that read as if they're written very easily and casually.

 Overwriting, Revision, Spontaneity, Structure

Alan Trustman

American screenwriter of The Thomas Crown Affair,
Bullitt, *and* They Call Me Mr. Tibbs!

The bigger the screen, the sharper your dialogue and the easier the rewrite. I use a 50 inch TV screen!

Dialogue, Revision, Screenwriting

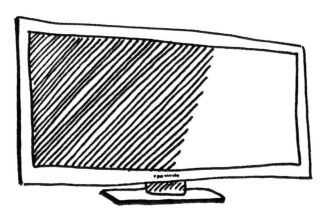

Andrew Vachss

American crime fiction writer and author of
the Burke *series of novels*

What is it you really want? Do you want to get published? Do you want to make your living out of it? Those are two different things. (Everyone says) read a lot... yeah, so what? If you read a lot, you're going to imitate? That's not the thing. To find your own voice is actually hard.

The two hardest things for a young writer are the actual craft, you know, the mechanics, and having something to write about.

Craft, Inspiration, Voice

Patty Volk

Novelist and essayist and author of Shocked,
White Light, *and* Stuffed

"Sometimes you can be working on a project and the muse lightening doesn't strike, but you sit down and you type anyway and I don't care what you write. That's what the garbage pail is for or what the file drawers are for. You just better write, because if you don't you're going to be in trouble.

 Determination, Inspiration

Karen Thompson Walker
Author of the novel The Age of Miracles

I think definitely patience, but not in the sense of patience with your own work. You have to just devote as much time whether that's hours or years to getting better before anything can happen with your writing. So to see people turn things in too early, and that happened. As an editor, I would see that or before they've really developed as a writer, I think that's something to avoid and definitely you have to be as perfectionist as possible on the sentence level and the story level as well.

Craft, Patience, Skill

David Foster Wallace
American novelist and MacArthur fellow and author of
Infinite Jest *and* **The Pale King**

The question divides into two areas. Very often students who come to grad programs are still into expressive writing, which is writing that is neat, by God; just because they're doing it and their teachers are encouraging them to do it and think it is interesting just because they're doing it. And I always want to give them a little bit of a taste of the grown-up reading world, which is really "they don't care about you." The reader has a very precious commodity, which is time and attention, and you're asking that reader for time and attention and you have to earn it. So very often, with students, my advice to them would be to try to expand their repertoire and do things that they don't do well. I notice that very often, writing students will come in with one or two things that they do particularly well, lyrical descriptions, for instance, or they are terrific at building a kind of emotional climax. But every single story will be the same, and I will be mean to them until they begin to try and do things that they don't believe they can do.

I sometimes also get letters from regular civilian people and they are often very moving, often from young men. And the tone is "I read such and such of yours and I really, really liked it and I, too, want to be a writer. And I don't know if you can help me, but is there some way that I can do stuff that I can be sure is as good and as likeable as I find your stuff?" And for some reason, these letters really get to me, and it is in writing back to some of these kids that I discover that what they're doing is they are afraid. They are afraid that they are going to invest themselves and they're going to invest their time and their stuff is not going to be any good. And they want to know if there's a formula, or technique; I mean, there's a whole industry of these "how-to" books that depend on this. And what I end up writing back to them is that I've got good news and I've got bad news.

The bad news is no there is no technique, and they had best learn to love this fear because it will be your companion for the rest of your life. The good news is that we all go through it and that if you want to keep doing this, the secret is not really so much to learn the secret techniques so you don't feel this fear anymore, but in fact to abide in this fear. Because the stuff, at least for me, that is difficult about writing is not the time and the work, because when it is going well, it is a labor of love... the hard thing is the fear. The fear that, "here's this thing that I've tried really hard on, and that I think is really good, and I'm going to give it to you and you're going to smile that kind of sickening polite smile and I'm going to be able to tell that you think it is excrement. And what is that going to say about me?" And at least in my experience, the fear never goes away.

 Audience, Fear, Love, Technique

Colson Whitehead

MacArthur Fellow, acclaimed novelist, and author of
The Intuitionist *and* **Zone One**

" Writing is a terrible job. You're going to get a lot of rejection and discouragement from the world, but the only person who's going to put the words on the page is you. So you're going to write something crappy, and next time it might be a little better and you've learned something. And then you'll have a relapse into complete crappiness, and then you'll try again, and so it's only by trying different things and discovering what kind of stuff you're good at, and then you have to keep going.

Career, Discouragement, Experimentation, Rejection, Tenacity

Tobias Wolff

O. Henry and PEN/Faulkner Award-winning author of
The Barracks Thief *and* **This Boy's Life**

Patience. To be patient with themselves. They should think of it as learning to play an instrument. They know, everybody knows, that you can't go into a music store and pick up a trumpet or saxophone and go home and in a couple of hours you're not going to be playing Coltrane or Sonny Rollins. It's not going to happen. However, if you stay with it for many years and you're patient with yourself, do your scales every day, and your breathing exercises, and learn your Alexander method and all that, someday you might sound pretty good. You might not sound like them but you might sound like yourself.

And yet we have this idea that since we can read and since we know generally all the words that the writers we like use, if you're not reading Nabokov, then we ought to be able to do that right away. So writers tend to get very impatient with themselves, young writers, and they ought to be as patient with themselves and give in and understand that time and practice are their friends, that sour notes are their friends because they're going to turn into sweet notes someday. That kind of patience is required of the writer just as it is as of the musician.

I listened to John Updike talking about writing over the radio not long ago and he was saying that sometimes writers are doing their best work even when they don't know they are doing their best work. And sometimes they're doing not very good work when they think they are doing great work, as they will see themselves later on. I know exactly what he's talking about. I think you just have to do it and later on you'll see how well you did it. But if you wait for it... I don't know any real writers who do that.

 Patience, Practice, Revision

Tom Wolfe

American New Journalism pioneer, novelist, and author of
The Right Stuff *and* **Bonfire of the Vanities**

 I can see why Sinclair Lewis was our first Nobel Prize winner—his work is absolutely brilliant. His literary stock has been sinking steadily since 1930 within the literary community, but he did something which I tried to do in *Bonfire*, which is probably why I'm so partial to him—he was a reporter. To do *Elmer Gantry*, which I think is his greatest book, he moved from New England to Cincinnati, he actually formed Bible Study classes for ministers so he could meet preachers. He gave sermons from pulpits during the summer, when ministers were all on vacation and they needed someone to fill in. He became an absolutely tireless reporter, much in the same way that Zola must have done. Zola used to call it "documenting" his novels.

Commitment, Immersion, Journalism, Research

William Zinsser

Author of the world-renowned On Writing Well

To think smart.

Strategy

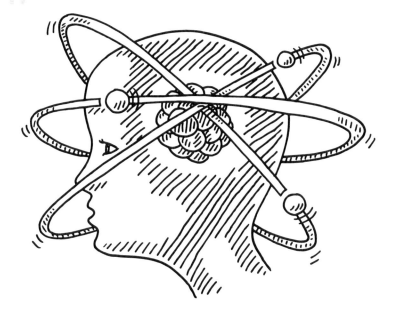

#TOPIC INDEX

ABOUT THE AUTHOR

Lewis Burke Frumkes hosts a weekly radio show on WPAT-AM and is the author of eight books, including *Favorite Words of Famous People*, *How to Raise Your I.Q. by Eating Gifted Children*, *The Logophile's Orgy*, *Manhattan Cocktail*, and *Metapunctuation*. His work has appeared in *Harper's*, *Punch*, and the *New York Times*. He is also the program director of the Writing Center - CE at Hunter College in New York. He lives in New York City.